P9-CAN-870

Class Trip

# SEATTLE

Claire O'Neal

Mitchell Lane
PUBLISHERS

P.O. Box 196
Hockessin, Delaware 19707
Visit us on the web: www.mitchelllane.com
Comments? email us: mitchelllane@mitchelllane.com

# Mitchell Lane
## PUBLISHERS

Boston • Chicago • New York City
Philadelphia • San Antonio • San Diego
**Seattle** • St. Augustine • Washington, D.C.

**Copyright © 2011 by Mitchell Lane Publishers**

All rights reserved. No part of this book may be reproduced without written permission from the publisher. Printed and bound in the United States of America.

**PUBLISHER'S NOTE:** The facts on which the story in this book are based have been thoroughly researched. Documentation of such research can be found on pages 44 and 45. While every possible effort has been made to ensure accuracy, the publisher will not assume liability for damages caused by inaccuracies in the data, and makes no warranty on the accuracy of the information contained herein.

**Printing** 1 2 3 4 5 6 7 8 9

**Library of Congress
Cataloging-in-Publication Data**

O'Neal, Claire.
  Class trip Seattle / by Claire O'Neal.
    p. cm. — (A Robbie reader)
  Includes bibliographical references and index.
  ISBN 978-1-58415-880-6 (library bound)
  1. Seattle (Wash.)—Description and travel—
Juvenile literature. 2. Seattle (Wash.)—History—
Juvenile literature. I. Title.
  F899.S44O54 2010
  917.9'7772—dc22                           2010000518

PLB

# CONTENTS

# SEATTLE

*This dramatic nighttime view of the Seattle skyline shows off the Space Needle, a symbol of the city since 1962.*

*Right: Speed skater Apolo Anton Ohno is the winner of the most U.S. Olympic medals (eight total) of all time. Ohno is a native of the Seattle suburb of Federal Way.*

# Seattle Surprise

You'd think it would be warmer, being May and all. School's almost out, but it's cool and rainy, like spring doesn't want to end. This morning as I stepped off the bus, the rain instantly found its way under my raincoat, into my shoes, everywhere. I think it's gross. My parents think it's awesome. "It reminds us of Seattle," my mom says, getting all moony in the eyes and rambling about salmon and cherry blossoms.

I'm Natalie. I'm in the fourth grade at West Park Elementary in Newark, Delaware. But I haven't lived in Delaware my whole life. I was actually born in Seattle, Washington. My parents lived there when they were students at the University of Washington. We left Seattle when my dad got a job here in Newark. I wasn't even two years old, so I don't remember a thing. Mom and Dad do, though. They miss it, and tell me stories about things we did when I was a baby.

"My favorite thing to do," Mom says, "was to take you for long walks in the city parks—along the lakeshore at Magnuson Park, on the path around Green Lake,

Green Lake in Seattle is a favorite gathering spot for geese and other wildlife. The lake's artificial island, built with dumped gravel, was turned into a wildlife reserve. It has been off limits to humans since 1952.

on the Burke-Gilman bike trail. I remember one sunny day, my whole office took a vacation day and went kayaking down the Lake Washington Canal! It was amazing how, even among huge skyscrapers, everything you saw seemed green and fresh."

"What about Dad?" I ask.

"Your dad loved the coffee!" Mom says, laughing. "Well, actually, he probably misses the mountains most. On a clear day, you could see peaks from the Cascade and the Olympic Mountains from just about anywhere in the city. We used to sit out on our patio with California rolls from his favorite **sushi** restaurant, watching the sun set on Mount Rainier. The mountains weren't just scenery to us, though. Dad and I went hiking on a different mountain every summer. I was always amazed by how close these enormous mountains were to the huge city."

"But doesn't it rain all the time there? How could you go hiking in the rain?"

Mom laughs again. "The rain? We just told that to the tourists so we could keep the city for ourselves! You may not know this, but it rains just as much here in Newark every year as it does in Seattle."

Now that did sound nice. I wish we could visit someday. Not likely, though. Seattle's about as far from Newark as you can be in the **continental** United States.

There's the bell! Time for school to start. Mr. Porter strolled in the classroom, his morning cup of Starbucks coffee in one hand.

A woman hiking in the Cascades has a spectacular view of Mount Rainier. Rainier is the highest peak in the Cascades, which stretch from northern California into British Columbia, Canada.

# Seattle

Washington

Seattle metronatural™

↑ To Woodland Park Zoo

SUB STATION

**SEATTLE CENTER**

Space Needle

Experience Music Project

OLYMPIC SCULPTURE PARK

Pier 70
Pier 69
Pier 67

Bell Harbor International Conference Center
Pier 66/Bell St. Cruise Terminal
Pier 62 & 63

Seattle Aquarium
Pier 59
Waterfront Park
Pier 57

**Elliott Bay**

Pier 56
Pier 55
Pier 54

Pier 52

**WA State Ferries**

Pier 48

Regrade Park

Steinbrueck Park

**PIKE PLACE MARKET**

Westlake Park

**Convention Center & Seattle Visitor Center**

Boren-Pike-Pine Park

**LIBRARY**

Freeway Park

City Hall Park
Pioneer Square Park
Occidental Square

Kobe Terrace Park

**PIONEER SQUARE**

King St. Station AMTRAK

Hing Hay Park

**CHINATOWN– INTERNATIONAL DISTRICT**
International Children's Park

Qwest Field (football)

Seahawks Exhibition Center

Safeco Field (baseball)

Royal Brougham Wy

## Streets and Avenues

Roy St, Mercer St, Republican St, Harrison St, Thomas St, John St, Denny Way, Mercer St

W Republican St, W Harrison St, W Thomas St, John St

1st Ave N, 2nd Ave N, Queen Anne Ave N, Taylor Ave N, 5th Ave N, 6th Ave N, Aurora Ave N

Dexter Ave N, 8th Ave N, 9th Ave N, Westlake Ave N, Terry Ave N, Boren Ave N, Fairview Ave N, Minor Ave N

Broad St, Clay St, Cedar St, Vine St, Wall St, Battery St, Bell St, Blanchard St, Lenora St, 1st Ave, 2nd Ave, 3rd Ave, 4th Ave, 5th Ave, 6th Ave, 7th Ave, 8th Ave, 9th Ave

Tilikum Place

Virginia St, Stewart St, Olive Way, Howell St, Minor Ave, Terry Ave, Broadway Ave

McGraw Square, Bus Terminal

Pine St, Pike St, Union St, University St, Seneca St, Spring St, Madison St, Marion St, Columbia St, Cherry St, James St, Alder St

Post Alley

Boylston Ave, Summit Ave, Boren Ave, Minor Ave, Terry Ave, 9th Ave, 8th Ave, 7th Ave, 6th Ave, 5th Ave, 4th Ave

Jefferson St, Terrace, Yesler Way

S Washington St, S Main St, S Jackson St, S King St, S Weller St, S Lane St, S Dearborn St

Occidental Ave S, 1st Ave S, 2nd Ave S, 3rd Ave S, 7th Ave S, Maynard Ave S

Elliott Avenue, Western Ave, Alaskan Way

I-5, 99

## Legend

- - - - - Free Ride Area
———— Monorail Route
▼········▲ South Lake Union Streetcar
■- - -■ Bus Tunnel & Stops
●————● Waterfront Streetcar Route

Pike Place Market to Qwest Event Center—1 mi / 1.6 km
Pike Place Market to Space Needle—1 mi / 1.6 km
Pike Place Market to Convention Center—½ mi / 800 m

■ Major Attractions
■ Parks

N
W · E
S

↓ Pier 30 Cruise Terminal
¾ mi / 1 km

"Good morning, class."

"Good morning, Mr. Porter."

"To wrap up our lessons on U.S. cities, we'll spend this week studying Seattle, Washington," Mr. Porter announced. I perk up. Seattle?

"Seattle is **unique** for a big city—it's one that really likes to mix work and play. You probably know that coffee giant Starbucks is headquartered there," he said, raising his white and green cup, "but did you also know that Native Americans have lived there for

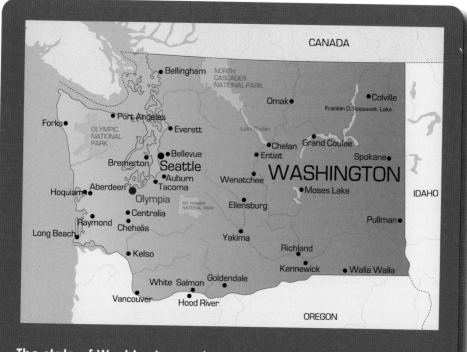

The state of Washington makes up the northwestern corner of the continental United States. Seattle lies on Puget Sound about 100 miles south of the U.S.-Canadian border. It is the northernmost major city in the country.

over 4,000 years? Or that the town began as a lumber mill? Or that it's the largest northernmost city in the continental United States?" We were all pretty impressed. It seemed as if we had a lot to learn about Seattle.

Coffee megachain Starbucks makes its headquarters in this old Sears and Roebuck catalog center in Seattle's SoDo neighborhood. Over 3,500 Starbucks employees work in the office building, which is the city's largest.

Careful, the beverage you're about to enjoy is extremely hot.

Mr. Porter continued, "We'll split the class into three groups. Each group will research and write a short report about the history, geography, or culture of Seattle. At the end of the week, we'll combine the three groups' work to make a guidebook for kids who want to visit the city."

At this, Mr. Porter grinned wide, as if he knew the punch line to a good joke. "Make sure you do a good job. We'll need the guidebook when we visit Seattle ourselves." Mr. P. waved a permission slip for us all to see, fanning the gasps of all the kids. "I've spoken with each of your parents to clear your schedules. We'll spend the last week of school there."

The whole class cheered! I turned around in my seat and high-fived my best friend Matthew. We were going on a class trip to Seattle!

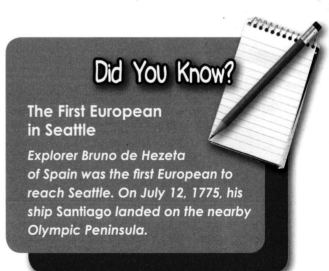

## Did You Know?

### The First European in Seattle

*Explorer Bruno de Hezeta of Spain was the first European to reach Seattle. On July 12, 1775, his ship Santiago landed on the nearby Olympic Peninsula.*

# SEATTLE

*The scenic Cascades Mountains to the east lure Seattleites away from town to hike during the summer and ski during the winter.*

*Right: Arthur Denny, the leader of the first group of non-Native Americans to settle in present-day Seattle*

# *Chapter* **2**

# New York—Someday

On November 13, 1851, a business-minded pioneer named Arthur Denny led twenty-two new settlers to Washington's Puget Sound. They were the first non-Native Americans to call Seattle home. In those days, adventurers and settlers from the East or the Midwest packed up and headed out on the Oregon Trail to start a new life on the rich farmland in the Oregon Territory. Few wanted to settle in the Washington Territory to the north. It seemed like an endless, rain-soaked forest until Denny recognized it as a business venture. He saw that with Puget Sound feeding into the Pacific Ocean, Washington's trees could supply lumber to the growing towns all along the West Coast.

Denny got help from Seattle's first residents, Native tribes such as the Hoh and Quileute. With the Natives, the new settlers built four log cabins before winter. In honor of their help—and of the Denny Party's sense of humor—Denny named the new city New York-*Alki*. *Alki* means "someday" in Chinook.

Chief Sealth was a Native leader who befriended early settlers in present-day Washington state. This statue of him stands in the middle of Seattle, the city that was named for him.

At Alki Point, the Denny Party endured a winter of storms, tides, and high winds. They moved across Elliott Bay in the spring, to a sheltered island surrounded by mud flats that would become downtown Seattle. They named the town after Chief Sealth, a Native leader and the settlers' friend. Once settled in their new home, they wasted no time starting up their new business. Henry Yesler built a steam-powered lumber mill on Elliott Bay in 1852. Seattleites chopped down trees on the high hills around town and simply slid the logs down "Skid Road" to the mill. At the same time, they cleared the land and used some of the lumber to construct streets, churches, and schools. They made a decent living trading the rest of their lumber to Oregon and California.

Also during this time, much of the American West was involved in the laying down of railroad lines connecting the West with other parts of the country. When the railroad work was finished, many people found themselves out of work. In the 1880s, with work in short supply, many Americans who had been working on the railroads turned their frustrations against Chinese immigrants who had also been encouraged to come to the United States to work on railroad crews.

Cutters strike a pose on, in, and around a tree while logging in the Cascades during the 1800s.

15

In 1885 and 1886, organized bands rioted against the Chinese community in Seattle, burning houses and shops and **intimidating** local Chinese residents. Fortunately, law enforcement officials restored order. Today Seattle has a large and diverse population of Chinese and other Asian Americans.

On June 6, 1889, a small fire began in a woodworking shop at Front Street and Madison Avenue. By the end of the day, The Great Seattle Fire had destroyed 25 blocks of the wooden city. Fortunately, only one person was known to have died as a direct result of the blaze, and determined Seattleites saw the fire as an opportunity. Residents rebuilt their city to last, this time out of brick, stone, and steel. They created the Denny Regrade, moving tons of dirt from the hills down to the streets, raising them out of the water's reach and making travel easier. The city's population grew from about 3,000 in 1880 to more

This stack of dishes was fused together during the Great Seattle Fire. It is on display at the Museum of History and Industry in Seattle.

The steamer *Rosalie* leaves Seattle with people seeking their fortune during the Klondike Gold Rush. Travelers passing through Seattle could rest, eat, and find supplies at new stores such as Nordstrom and Eddie Bauer.

than 40,000 in 1890, thanks to its new beauty and can-do spirit.

The ship *Portland* arrived in Seattle from Alaska on July 17, 1897, loaded with what was described as a "ton of gold." Hearing the news, tens of thousands of people around the world left their jobs and homes to become **prospectors**, mining for gold in the Klondike region of Canada, east of Alaska. Seattle became a major stopping point on the long journey north.

Some historians suggest that half of the gold found in the Klondike was spent in Seattle. Some prospectors liked the city so much they decided to stay. Seattle

17

Seattle hosted the World's Fair in 1962. For the occasion, the city built the Pacific Science Center (above), the first science museum in the United States. Also built was the Space Needle (shown at right next to the statue of Chief Sealth).

quickly became a mixed bag of cultures, especially attracting Scandinavian and Chinese immigrants. They worked in new Seattle industries such as iron mills, shipbuilding, and railroading. They also created Seattle's distinct neighborhoods. By 1910, Seattle was the biggest city in the Pacific Northwest, boasting a population of 250,000 and growing.

In 1916, William Boeing and Clyde Esterveld began their company, and a new Seattle era, with a home-built **pontoon** plane launched from Lake Union. During World War II, Boeing built hundreds of bombers each month and attracted huge numbers of workers to the city. By 1945, Seattle's population had grown to over 500,000.

Seattle's next big idea came in the 1990s, when Seattle natives Bill Gates and Paul Allen built the software giant Microsoft near their hometown. Young Microsoft employees became instant millionaires during the company's boom in the 1990s and early 2000s, flooding the city with money. Microsoft's success attracted other hi-tech companies like Nintendo, RealNetworks, and Amazon.com. Meanwhile, poor Seattle kids turned to their basements, guitars in hand, to let their frustration out in music. They created the **grunge rock** movement in the 1990s, and made Seattle's music scene world famous for plaid shirts, distorted guitar sounds, and depressing lyrics.

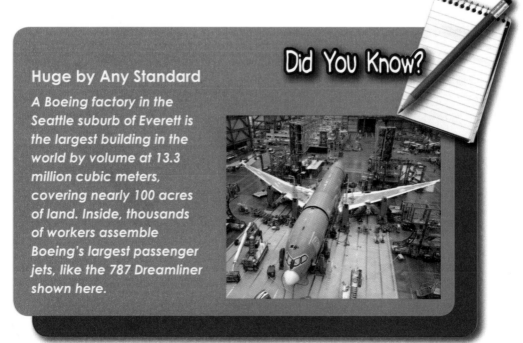

Did You Know?

**Huge by Any Standard**

*A Boeing factory in the Seattle suburb of Everett is the largest building in the world by volume at 13.3 million cubic meters, covering nearly 100 acres of land. Inside, thousands of workers assemble Boeing's largest passenger jets, like the 787 Dreamliner shown here.*

# SEATTLE

*Viewed from the air, the buildings and streets of Seattle seem to weave in and out of green parklands and blue waters.*

*Right: Many native Seattleites gave up umbrellas long ago, preferring **high-tech** waterproof jackets, slickers, or just hats.*

*Chapter*

# 3

# Around the Emerald City

The city of Seattle is an **isthmus**, a narrow strip of land that separates two bodies of water. To its west is Puget Sound, an arm of the Pacific Ocean that reaches into the northwestern corner of Washington state. To Seattle's east is Lake Washington. These natural boundaries restrict the city's borders. However, suburbs sprawl out from Seattle to Bellevue in the north, Tacoma in the south, and Redmond in the east. As of 2009, Seattle counted 602,200 residents, making it the most populous city in Washington state. Add in the suburbs to get the thirteenth most populated U.S. metro area, at 3,524,000 people. Fortunately, engineers have found creative ways to help the flow of people around Seattle's bodies of water.

Seattle has a famous reputation as a rainy town. On average, it sees 36.2 inches of **precipitation** each year. Compare this, however, to the annual average precipitation in other major U.S. cities. New York City (40.3 inches), Atlanta (49 inches), Boston (44 inches), and Houston (45 inches)—they all get more! The

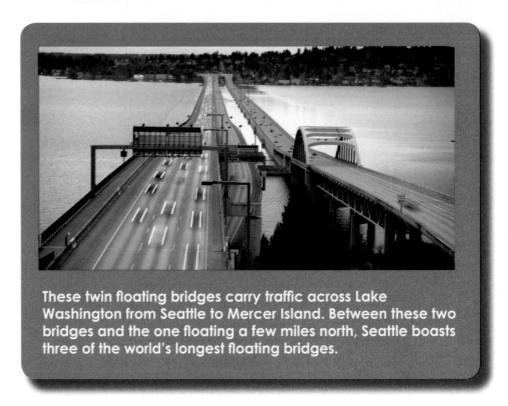

These twin floating bridges carry traffic across Lake Washington from Seattle to Mercer Island. Between these two bridges and the one floating a few miles north, Seattle boasts three of the world's longest floating bridges.

difference is that, in these other cities, precipitation occurs mostly in heavy rainstorms or blizzards. In Seattle, precipitation falls gradually between October and April each year.

Seattle's winter is wet and cloudy, but rarely freezing. Typical high temperatures reach the 40s in January and February. Fall and spring bring a bit more sunshine and warmer temperatures, with average highs in the 60s in both April and October. Seattleites wait all year for their glorious summers. With low **humidity**, clear skies, typical high temperatures in July and August barely breaking 80°F, and the sun staying out until nearly 10:00 P.M., you'll catch Seattleites taking extra days off from work when summer comes around.

One of Seattle's nicknames is "The Emerald City," and it's easy to see why. Thanks to the rain and mild temperatures, forests of hemlock, Douglas fir, and red cedar cover the city in a blanket of year-round green. This beauty is showcased in 6,200 acres of parks and public gardens, 11 percent of Seattle's total land area. Many parks help make otherwise wasted land environmentally friendly. Two parks, Discovery Park

The International Fountain was originally part of the Seattle World's Fair in 1962. Today it still attracts crowds of Seattleites and visitors alike, especially on summer days.

Gas Works Park turned the area surrounding this old natural gas plant into a beautiful space. Here, people can fly kites or watch boats on Elliott Bay.

and Magnuson Park, reuse buildings from abandoned Army and Navy bases.

Every hilltop in town treats a visitor to sweeping views of sparkling water in all directions, the dazzling white of the glacier-capped Cascade Mountains to the north and south, and the Olympic Mountain Range to the west. The peak of Mount Rainier, the tallest in the **contiguous** United States at 14,411 feet, is only 60 miles southeast of Seattle.

"The Mountain" and its neighbors are actually slumbering volcanoes. Seattle lies on the Ring of Fire—a pattern of volcanoes and earthquakes bordering the Pacific. Mount St. Helens, 96 miles south of Seattle, erupted on May 18, 1980, killing 57 and dumping ash all over the Pacific Northwest.

## Did You Know?

### A Glacier of Epic Proportions

Roughly 17,000 years ago, an enormous, 4-mile-high sheet of ice known as the Vashon **Glacier** covered Seattle. The Vashon carved out Seattle's seven hills, Puget Sound, and Lake Washington before melting 13,000 years ago. Lake Washington is shown here, with Mercer Island connected to Seattle by side-by-side floating bridges.

# SEATTLE

*A seaplane and a kayak meet on Elliott Bay. Boating and aviation shaped Seattle's history. Today, they continue to bring people to the city, for work and play.*

*Right: Pirates liven up the springtime Seafair festival. They also perform year-round acts of community service.*

# Coffee Culture

Rain or shine, the Emerald City has a lot to offer, especially outdoors. You can bike on the Burke-Gilman Trail, skate around Green Lake, or kayak across Elliott Bay. One in six Seattleites owns a boat, more per person than any other U.S. city. They celebrate the beginning of boating season in June with a month-long festival called Seafair. Hydrofoil races on Lake Washington—think NASCAR with boats—end Seafair with a splash. Meanwhile, the glistening mountains lie only two hours away, calling out to everyone who enjoys a great hike.

When foul weather hits, as it often does in the winter, Seattleites gather in their favorite coffee shops to work, study, and surf the Internet. As the birthplace of coffee megachain Starbucks (you can visit the first Starbucks in Pike Place Market), Seattle is sometimes known as the Coffee Capital of America. It's easy to understand coffee's appeal here. Seattle lies so far north that the winter sun doesn't come up until 7:30 A.M. and sets as early as 4:30 P.M. The short, dark days and long winter

Hydrofoil racers on Lake Washington bring speed and thrills to the close of Seafair.

rains call out for good coffee. Still, with great skiing waiting in the mountains, even dark winter days can't stop outdoor plans.

The gorgeous scenery fuels creativity, making Seattle an artsy town. Seattle's performing arts scene includes the Seattle Symphony, the Seattle Opera, and the Pacific Northwest Ballet. Seattleites especially

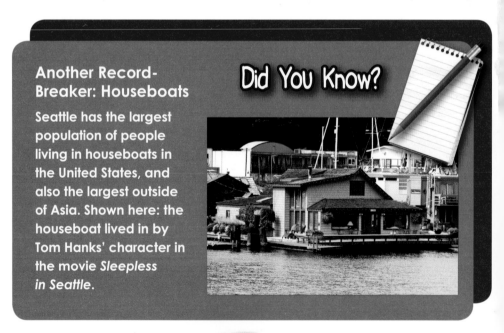

**Another Record-Breaker: Houseboats**

**Did You Know?**

Seattle has the largest population of people living in houseboats in the United States, and also the largest outside of Asia. Shown here: the houseboat lived in by Tom Hanks' character in the movie *Sleepless in Seattle*.

**This sign promotes two of Pike Place Market's most famous products—coffee and fresh fish.**

enjoy their music outdoors, flocking to the Northwest Folklife Festival over Memorial Day weekend and Bumbershoot over Labor Day weekend.

Seattle also inspires with several art museums and the outdoor Olympic Sculpture Park on the waterfront. But perhaps Seattle's art is most fun on the street. Public sculptures and statues are found in unexpected places, and even some of the buildings downtown look like works of art, such as the Seattle Public Library, designed by Dutch architect Rem Koolhas, and the Experience Music Project, a music museum designed by architect Frank O. Gehry.

Seattleites root for several sports teams. Many are serious fans when it comes to the University of Washington Huskies football team. Major League

One of Seattle's favorite sons—guitar legend Jimi Hendrix—was born and raised near Skid Road, an area where lumber once slid downhill to a sawmill.

Baseball's Mariners play at Safeco Field, which has a retractable roof to guard against rain delays. The NFL's Seahawks play football at Qwest Field. Seattle sports suffered a blow when the NBA Seattle Supersonics were sold and moved to Oklahoma City in 2008. However, Key Arena continues to house the 2004 WNBA champions, the Seattle Storm. In 2009, Seattle added a pro soccer team—the Sounders—to its sports roster.

Seattleites work just as hard as they play. Since World War II, the single-largest employer in the Seattle area has been air- and spacecraft company Boeing. Other nationally important businesses headquartered in the Seattle area include cell phone provider T-Mobile, warehouse retailer Costco, camping and hiking retailer R.E.I., and lumber giant Weyerhaeuser. Biomedical research is also booming in Seattle, with major centers at the University of Washington, the Fred Hutchinson Cancer Research Institute, and the Seattle Children's Hospital.

Getting around the touristy parts of Seattle is a breeze, with Seattle's wide sidewalks and free buses downtown. But to really get to know Seattle, visit the different neighborhoods, each with its own style. These very different personalities, all living together, are what really makes this Emerald City shine.

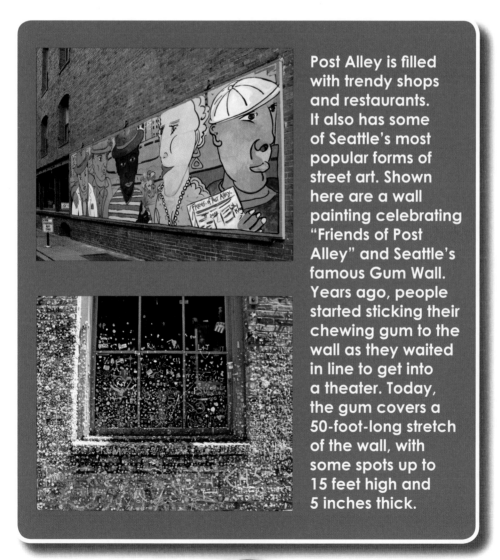

Post Alley is filled with trendy shops and restaurants. It also has some of Seattle's most popular forms of street art. Shown here are a wall painting celebrating "Friends of Post Alley" and Seattle's famous Gum Wall. Years ago, people started sticking their chewing gum to the wall as they waited in line to get into a theater. Today, the gum covers a 50-foot-long stretch of the wall, with some spots up to 15 feet high and 5 inches thick.

# SEATTLE

Pike Place Market is known for its lively, colorful atmosphere and incredible assortment of fresh seafood.

Right: Toucans are among the many species of tropical birds and other animals at the Woodland Park Zoo in Fremont.

# My Trip to Seattle

It's Monday, and here we are in Seattle! Everybody was amazed by the views—mountains, water, and trees everywhere! If it weren't for the skyscrapers, you could almost forget you were in a big city. Our first stop was Pike Place Market, a famous public marketplace that has been open since 1907. We strolled the open-air shops, ducking and laughing as workers from the Flying Fish Company hurled their freshly caught wares through the air right in front of us. Street musicians played live music as we took in the sights—fresh flowers, magic shops, seafood galore, and, of course, the first Starbucks coffee shop.

Tuesday we took a two-minute ride on the Monorail to Seattle Center. The observation deck of the Space Needle, 520 feet in the sky, treated us to breathtaking views of the entire city, as well as the bays, lakes, and mountains that surrounded us.

From above, the Experience Music Project looked like a rumpled metal quilt. Inside it was more about metal music! The museum has collected over 80,000

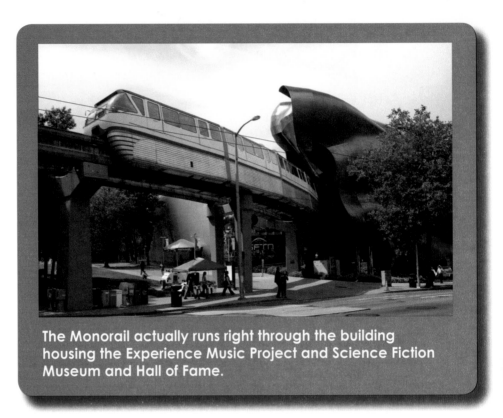

The Monorail actually runs right through the building housing the Experience Music Project and Science Fiction Museum and Hall of Fame.

artifacts from music history, like Jimi Hendrix's guitars, handwritten lyrics from 1990s grunge bands like Nirvana, and stage costumes from girl-powered rock band Heart. Next we visited the Pacific Science Center, the first science and technology museum in the United States. We loved the moving, roaring dinosaurs, the virtual-reality basketball game, and blasting targets with water cannons. We ended our night with a 7:00 show of *The Brementown Musicians* at the Seattle Children's Theater.

On Wednesday morning, a small cruise boat took us across Puget Sound for a visit to Tillicum Village, a recreated Native American settlement. We ate some delicious clam soup and fire-roasted salmon, seeing how tribes here have lived on the bounty of the sea. We walked on the beach, crunching clamshells beneath our feet. After exploring life above the sea, we headed back to town and met the creatures that live in and around Washington's waters—from sea otters to salmon to shorebirds—at the Seattle Aquarium.

The Seattle Art Museum's amazing collection of paintings and sculptures awaited us on Thursday, when admission was free. Afterward, we headed to Pioneer Square, Seattle's original downtown. There the Klondike Gold Rush Museum was built to show how people lived during the days of discovery. We ended our day with Thai food and shopping in the International

The Experience Music Project is impressive even from the outside, especially when lit up at dusk.

The visitors' center of Tillicum Village is modeled after a longhouse. It contains exhibits, food, and artifacts that reflect past and present Native culture in the Pacific Northwest.

District. I bought some Chinese tea for my mom from Uwajimaya, a famous—and enormous!—Asian grocery store.

We traveled just north of downtown Seattle to Ballard on Friday, my favorite day of the whole trip. I watched the boats come and go at the Hiram M. Chittenden Locks, which connect the freshwater Lake Washington with the saltwater Puget Sound. Salmon have trouble getting in and out of the locks, so the Army Corps of Engineers built a 21-step ladder for them. We saw the fish actually jumping up these steps, sometimes so high that they shot out of the water!

Next up was the nearby Nordic Heritage Museum. "Imagine you are a Scandinavian immigrant in the

1900s," Mr. Porter said. "What was it like to leave your home and cross not just the Atlantic but also North America, to settle in Seattle?"

We began our Saturday at the Woodland Park Zoo in Fremont. You won't find many cages here! This zoo is a world leader in re-creating its animals' natural habitats. My favorite was the African **savannah**. The giraffes ate right out of my hand! Next, we went statue hunting around Fremont, a fun, funky neighborhood. We ended the day at Gas Works Park, taking turns flying Mr. Porter's kite and watching the sun set across Elliott Bay on downtown Seattle.

Sunday, we visited the University District. At the Burke Museum, we learned about the dinosaurs, glaciers, and ancestors of today's Native tribes that were once in Washington state. After a tasty lunch at Agua Verde Café on the canal, Mr. Porter led us around back to their kayak shop. We put on lifejackets, partnered up, and spent the afternoon kayaking the Arboretum, a natural preserve in the heart of the city. The ducks seemed to follow us back to our dinner at Ivar's Salmon House under the I-5 highway bridge. We ate out on

*Seattle Art Museum*

**The Fremont Troll is a 16-foot-tall statue of a troll living under a bridge, crushing a real car with his hand!**

the patio next to the canal. Monday was our last day in Seattle. We hopped on a bus to SeaTac airport, and Mr. Porter surprised us one more time: "One last stop before home, kids. The Boeing Museum of Flight." This place was huge! It took us all morning to wind through exhibits of every age of flight, from Leonardo da Vinci's plans in the Middle Ages to space travel. There were twenty full-sized planes hanging from the ceiling of the Great Gallery. In the life-sized control tower, we each got a turn piloting a jet using a real flight **simulator** program.

That afternoon we took our turn being passengers— on our flight home. I couldn't believe all the things we had seen and done in a week. As we flew over Mount Rainier, I looked out the window and realized that we'd had so much fun in Seattle that we hadn't even gotten to the mountains. Maybe next time we'd get in a hike, like real Seattleites.

# Just The Facts

**Founded:** November 13, 1851

**Area:** 84 square miles

**Form of Government:** Mayor and nine-member City Council

**Seattle Population (City):** 602,200 (2009 census estimate)

**Greater Seattle Area Population (Metropolitan Area):** 3,524,000 (2007 census estimate)

**Population Density:** 6,979 people per square mile

**Percent of Population Under 18:** 15.6%

**Percent of Population That Are College Graduates:** 47.2% (highest in the United States)

**U.S. Rank:** 23rd most populous city; 13th most populous metro area

**Latitude:** 47° 39' north

**Longitude:** 122° 17' west

**Highest Point:** 520 feet, near the water tower at 35th Ave SW and SW Myrtle Street.

**Lowest Point:** sea level

**Average High:** 59°F

**Average Low:** 44°F

**Highest Recorded Temperature:** 103°F on July 29, 2009

**Lowest Recorded Temperature:** 0°F on January 31, 1950

**Average Annual Precipitation:** 36.2 inches

**Major Neighborhoods:** Ballard, Capitol Hill, Downtown, First Hill, Fremont, Green Lake, International District, Queen Anne, University District

**Major League Sports Teams:** Mariners—Baseball; Seahawks—Football; Storm—WNBA Basketball; Sounders—Soccer

**Major Museums and Cultural Centers:** Benaroya Hall, McCaw Hall, Pike Place Market, Seattle Art Museum, Seattle Center

**Major Daily Newspapers:** *Seattle Post-Intelligencer* (online only); *Seattle Times*

**City Mottoes:** "City of Flowers" and "City of Goodwill"

**City Bird:** Great Blue Heron

**City Flower:** *Dahlia*

# CRAFT TIME

## Make a Rain Gauge

Seattle's rains make Seattle green. Do you get a lot of rain where you live? You can make your own rain gauge to measure precipitation.

### What You Need:

Small, straight-sided clear cup or
   jar (like for pickles, olives, or jelly)
Permanent marker
Ruler
Wire coat hanger (optional)
Notebook

## What You Do:

1   Set the ruler upright inside the cup so that the beginning of the ruler is at the bottom of the jar.

2   Using the permanent marker, copy the markings on the ruler onto the inside wall of the cup.

3   Set the cup outside on a flat surface. Choose a location away from roofs, large trees, or anything that might prevent the cup from catching rain. You can also hang your rain gauge by bending a wire hanger around it.

4   Wait for a storm. Measure the water caught by your rain gauge.

5   Check your measurement against the local weather station, or online at www.weather.com.

6   Keep a notebook with your rain measurements over time. Measure precipitation for a month, and compare your rainfall with monthly averages for Seattle at www.weather.com/weather/wxclimatology/monthly/graph/USWA0395.

# Seattle Timeline

**1775**    On July 12, explorer Bruno de Hezeta claims the Pacific Northwest in the name of Spain.

**1770s**   One-third of the West Coast Native population dies from smallpox carried by European settlers.

**1792**    British Royal Navy Captain George Vancouver explores Puget Sound during his travels among the waterways of the Pacific Northwest, claiming it for Great Britain. He gives it the name "Puget's Sound" in honor of one of his officers.

**1841**    Puget Sound is officially named by British surveyor Charles Wilkes.

**1851**    On November 13, Arthur Denny leads a group of twenty-two settlers, including his family and friends, to Alki Point. The so-called Denny Party becomes the first group of non-Native residents of the Seattle area.

**1853**    The U.S government creates Washington Territory.

**1861**    Asa Mercer founds the University of Washington.

**1864**    Seattle becomes "connected" to the rest of the country when it receives its first transcontinental telegraph.

**1866**    Chief Sealth, a Native leader who befriended   and cooperated with white settlers—and for whom Seattle was named—dies.

**1875**    San Francisco begins regular steamship service to Seattle.

**1881**    Henry Yesler opens Seattle's first sawmill during the "boom" period of the logging industry. The path leading down to his mill, along which logs were slid, became known as Skid Road.

**1889**    On June 6, the Great Seattle Fire burns much of the city's center to the ground.

**1897**    On July 17, the Klondike Gold Rush begins. Seattle becomes the major port for gold prospectors headed north to Canada.

**1907**    Pike Place Market is founded. The world's first gas station opens in Seattle, at the corner of Holgate Street and Western Avenue.

**1916**    William Boeing and Clyde Esterveld launch their first plane from Lake Union. As Boeing's aircraft operation grows, the company bearing his name will employ hundreds of thousands of engineers, scientists, and other workers, and the Seattle area will become known for its role in the aerospace and defense aircraft industries.

**1940**    The Mercer Island pontoon (floating) bridge opens, allowing the city to expand to the east.

**1962**    Seattle hosts the World's Fair, building the Space Needle and the Pacific Science Center for the occasion.

**1969**    Major league baseball expands into Seattle, giving the city its first big-league team, the Pilots. After a disastrous season on the field and at the gate, the team is sold and moves to become the Milwaukee Brewers days before the 1970 season begins.

**1971**    The first Starbucks Coffee shop opens in Pike Place Market.

**1977**    Major league baseball returns to Seattle with another expansion team, the Mariners.

**1999**    Safeco Field opens as the new home of the Mariners.

**2000**    The downtown Kingdome is demolished to make room for the new Seahawks Stadium, completed two years later. The Experience Music Project opens.

**2001**    On February 28, a magnitude 6.8 earthquake rocks Seattle, damaging many of the original buildings in Pioneer Square.

**2004**    The Seattle Central Library opens downtown, featuring a unique design by world-famous Dutch architect Rem Koolhas.

**2007**    The Olympic Sculpture Park opens.

**2008**    The Supersonics of the National Basketball Association leave Seattle to become the Oklahoma City Thunder.

**2009**    On March 17, the *Seattle Post-Intelligencer* ceases its print operation and becomes an online-only publication, leaving Seattle with only one major daily newspaper, the *Seattle Times*, in print. On July 29, Seattle's highest temperature—103°F—is recorded.

# Further Reading

## Books

Bergman, Ann, and Virginia Smith. *Out and About with Kids: Seattle*. Seattle: Sasquatch Books, 2005.

Burton, Joan. *Best Hikes with Kids in Western Washington and the Cascades*. Seattle: The Mountaineers, 2006.

## Internet Sources

I Am Seattle. http://www.spaceneedle.com/iamseattle/index.html

Seattle Convention and Visitor's Bureau. http://www.visitseattle.org/visitors/

Seattle Virtual Tour. http://www.seattle.gov/tour/default.htm

Washington State Field Guide. http://www.washington.edu/burkemuseum/fieldguide/index.php

## Works Consulted

Bergman, Donna. *Kids Go! Seattle*. Santa Fe: John Muir Publications, 1996.

Dickey, J. D., and Richie Unterberger. *The Rough Guide to Seattle*. New York: Rough Guides, 2003.

Jones, Jana. "Taking the Kids: Three Days in Seattle." *The Independent Traveler*. http://www.independenttraveler.com/resources/article.cfm?AID=581&category=32

Lange, Greg. "Smallpox epidemic ravages Native Americans on the northwest coast of North America in the 1770s." *HistoryLink.org*, January 23, 2003. http://www.historylink.org/index.cfm?DisplayPage=output.cfm&file_id=5100

Longenbaugh, John. *Insight Pocket Guide: Seattle*. Long Island City, NY: Langenscheidt Publishers, 2006.

Ohlsen, Becky. *Seattle City Guide*. Oakland: Lonely Planet Publications Pty, Ltd., 2008.

Samson, Karl. *Frommer's Seattle*. Hoboken, NJ: Wiley Publishing, 2008.

Samson, Karl. *Frommer's Washington State*. Hoboken, NJ: Wiley Publishing, 2008.

Sanchez, Antonio. "Bruno de Hezeta (Heceta) party lands at future site of Grenville Bay and claims the Pacific Northwest for Spain on July 12, 1775." *History Link.org*, April 22, 2004. http://www.historylink.org/index.cfm?DisplayPage=output.cfm&file_id=5690

Seattle City Office of Intergovernmental Relations. *The Greater Seattle Data Sheet*. http://www.seattle.gov/oir/datasheet/

Seattle Monorail Official Homepage. http://www.seattlemonorail.com/index.php

Seattle Parks and Recreation Home Page. http://www.seattle.gov/parks/

See Seattle Walking Tours and Events. http://www.see-seattle.com

Sisson, Thomas W. "History and Hazards of Mount Rainier, Washington." Mount Rainier National Park's Official Homepage. http://www.nps.gov/archive/mora/ncrd/hazards.htm

Space Needle. http://www.spaceneedle.com/

Tedesko, Suzanne. *Seattle's 25 Best*. New York: Fodor's Travel Publications, 2008. University of Washington Libraries. "The Great Seattle Fire." http://content.lib.washington.edu/extras/seattle-fire.html.

Watson, Kenneth Greg. "Chief Seattle." HistoryLink.org, January 18, 2003. http://www.historylink.org/index.cfm?DisplayPage=output.cfm&file_id=5071

# Glossary

**contiguous**—Next to or together in sequence; touching or sharing a border (example: the contiguous forty-eight U.S. states).

**continental**—Forming or belonging to a continent.

**glacier** (GLAY-shur)—A slowly moving mass of ice formed over thousands or millions of years by compacted snow.

**grunge rock**—A type of rock music that developed in the Seattle area in the 1980s. The term *grunge* also refers to the type of fashion associated with grunge rock.

**high-tech**—Produced by or having to do with advanced forms of technology; very modern.

**humidity**—The amount of water vapor in the atmosphere.

**intimidating**—Frightening or threatening others, especially in order to get them to do something a certain way.

**isthmus** (ISTH-muhs)—A narrow strip of land with water on either side, connecting two larger areas of land.

**pontoon**—A hollow cylinder used to float or support a boat or some other structure, such as a bridge.

**precipitation** (pree-sip-uh-TAY-shun)—Rain, snow, sleet, or hail that falls to the ground.

**prospectors**—People who search for gold or some other mineral, usually by digging or drilling.

**savannah** (suh-VAN-uh)—(often spelled *savanna*) A grassy plain in a tropical or subtropical region, usually with few trees.

**simulator** (SIM-yoo-lay-tur)—A machine with a set of controls and conditions designed to create an experience similar to operating a complicated piece of equipment.

**sushi** (SOO-shee)—A Japanese dish consisting of rolls of cold cooked rice containing fish or vegetables.

**unique** (yoo-NEEK)—very special or unusual; the only one of its kind.

PHOTO CREDITS: Cover (top left), pp. 10, 11, 13, 16, 18, 19, 20, 24–25 (top), 25 (bottom), 27, 30, 31 (bottom), 35, 36, 37, 38, back cover (inset)—Wikipedia (public domain); cover (top right), cover (bottom), pp. 4, 5, 6, 7, 9, 12, 14, 21, 22, 23, 26, 28, 29, 31 (top), 32, 33, 34, back cover (main)—Shutterstock; p. 8—Seattle's Convention and Visitors Bureau; pp. 15, 17—Library of Congress. Every effort has been made to locate all copyright holders of material used in this book. If any errors or omissions have occurred, corrections will be made in future editions of the book.

# Index

# ABOUT THE AUTHOR

A versatile author, Claire O'Neal has written over a dozen books with Mitchell Lane, including *Washington, D.C.* from this series. She holds degrees in English and Biology from Indiana University, and a Ph.D. in Chemistry from the University of Washington. Claire lived in Seattle for four and a half years. She especially enjoyed taking walks in Seattle's many parks, or going for hikes in the mountains nearby. She now lives in Delaware with her husband, two young sons, and a fat black cat.